Ecosystems

William B. Rice

Consultants

Sally Creel, Ed.D.
Curriculum Consultant

Leann Iacuone, M.A.T., NBCT, ATC
Riverside Unified School District

Image Credits: p.9 iStock; p.14 (bottom) Andrew J. Martinez/Science Source; p.7 (top) Douglas Faulkner/Science Source; p.16 (center) John Mitchell/Science Source; p.15 (top) Len Rue, Jr./Science Source; pp.28–29 (illustrations) Janelle Bell-Martin; all other images from Shutterstock.

Library of Congress Cataloging-in-Publication Data

Rice, William B. (William Benjamin), 1961- author.
Ecosystems / William B. Rice ; consultant, Sally Creel, Ed.D., curriculum consultant, Leann Iacuone, M.A.T., NBCT, ATC, Riverside Unified School District, Jill Tobin, California Teacher of the Year semi-finalist, Burbank Unified School District.
pages cm
Summary: "Living and nonliving things live together, in an ecosystem. Each thing living in the ecosystem relies on something else. To stay alive, all living things in an ecosystem need to live in balance. Can you think of an ecosystem you have seen?"— Provided by publisher.
Audience: K to grade 3.
Includes index.
ISBN 978-1-4807-4600-8 (pbk.)
ISBN 978-1-4807-5067-8 (ebook)
1. Biotic communities—Juvenile literature.
2. Ecology—Juvenile literature. I. Title.
QH541.14.R488 2015
577—dc23

2014014109

Teacher Created Materials
5301 Oceanus Drive
Huntington Beach, CA 92649-1030
http://www.tcmpub.com

ISBN 978-1-4807-4600-8

Printed in China WAI002

Table of Contents

Earth: The Life Planet

People have been all over Earth. They have been in every type of **condition**. They have seen every type of land. They have been in fierce heat. They have been in raging storms. They have seen land that is soggy. They have seen land that is bone dry.

These emperor penguins live in freezing Antarctica.

Every place they go, people find one thing: life. Earth is filled with life. In fact, it is the only planet we know that has life on it.

Lizards enjoy the dry heat of the desert.

Scuba divers swim deep in the oceans.

People study Earth and all it holds. We study the land, water, and air. We have learned plants and animals are alive. We know they use both living and nonliving things to survive.

Models help us see how things work. One kind of model is a **hierarchy** (HAHY-uh-rahr-kee). It ranks groups of things together. In nature, it ranks from smallest to largest.

Nonliving Helpers

Living things use nonliving things such as soil, water, air, and sunlight to survive.

This scientist studies a manatee to learn more about the ocean.

This scientist tests water to see how clean it is.

What groups are in the hierarchy of life? An **organism** is a single living thing. It is part of a population. That is a group of other things like itself. A population is part of a community. That is all the populations in an area. Communities and nonliving things in an area make an **ecosystem** (EE-koh-sis-tuhm).

Organisms

Every living thing is an organism. Oak trees, ravens, spiders, raspberry bushes, mountain lions, and humans are all organisms.

ecosystem
community
population
organism

What Does It Mean?

Ecosystem is a big word! It is really two words in one. The first part comes from the word *ecology*. That is the study of living things in their home. It looks at how they use soil, water, and the sun.

A lynx has long fur to keep it warm in the snow of the forests of America, Europe, and Asia.

Sea turtles live in almost every ocean in the world.

Many mongooses live in burrows in Africa.

Human bodies have a system that gets oxygen and **nutrients** to the entire body.

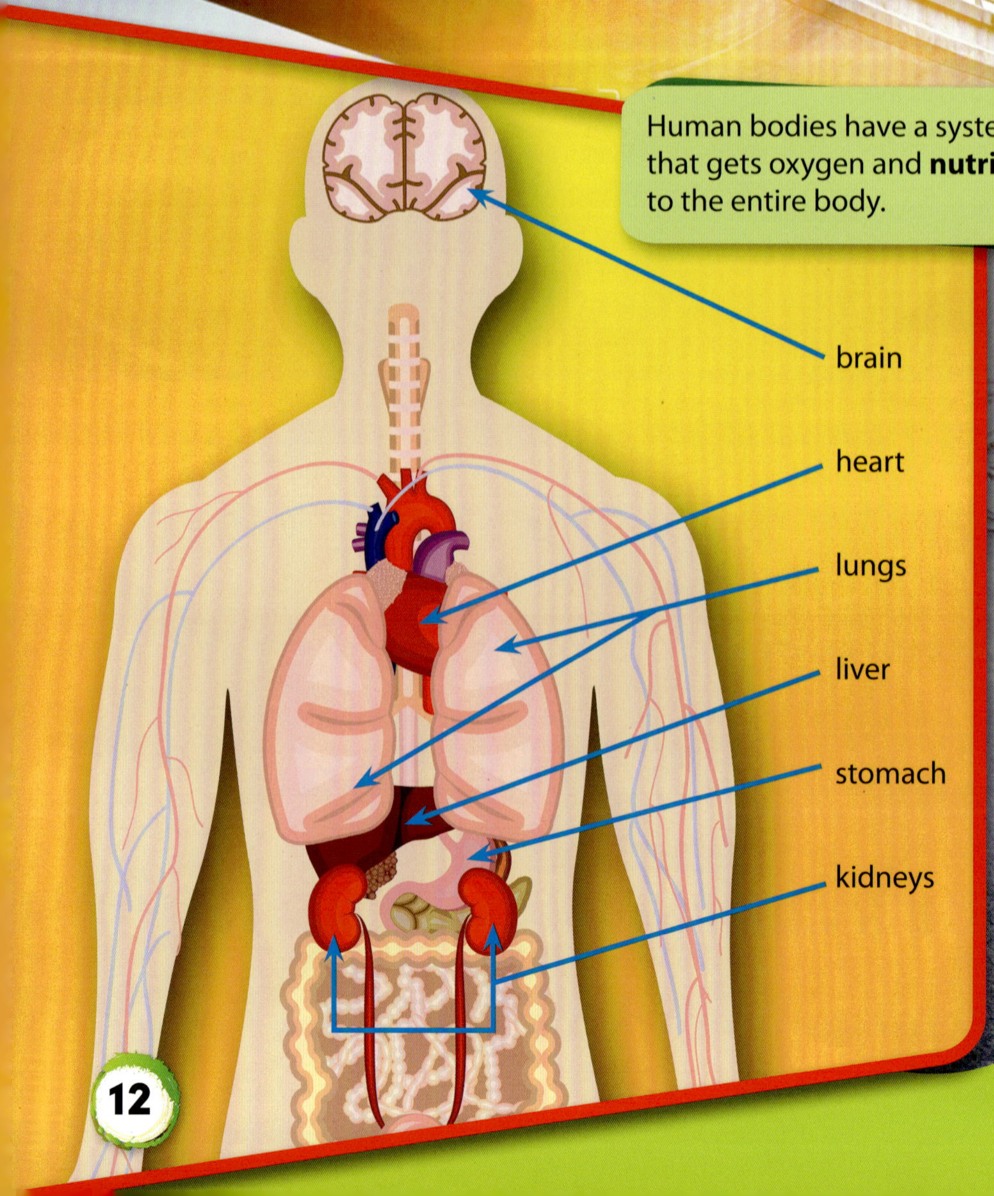

The second part of the word is *system*. A system is a group of parts working together. Our roads are one kind of system. The human body is another kind.

Put the two words together. An *ecosystem* is everything that lives in a certain place. It includes how living things use soil, water, and the sun. It also includes the way living things interact with one another.

Roads and highways create a system for connecting cities and towns.

Parts of Ecosystems

All living things need **energy**. Most plants get energy from the sun. They use the sun's light to make food. They also use nutrients from the soil. We call plants **producers**. They produce, or make, food on their own.

Some living things get their energy from other living things. They eat them. We call them **consumers**. They eat, or consume, plants or animals.

This sea raven eats a crab. It is a consumer.

Lions are consumers. They eat other animals to get energy.

A rabbit is a consumer. It eats plants.

Grass is a producer.

Some living things get their energy from dead things. We call them **decomposers**. They decompose, or break down, living things that have died. They are mainly very small things, such as fungi. Producers can use what decomposers leave behind to make their food.

Fungi

Fungi (FUHN-gahy) are very small organisms that usually live in soil. Mushrooms are the fruit of a certain group of fungi.

There are a lot of decomposers in a swamp.

The molds on these fruits are types of fungi. They are decomposers.

Have you ever walked by a stinky trash can? That is the smell of decomposition!

mushrooms

These birds eat ticks off this baby ram.

All the living things in an ecosystem depend on one another. They are in **balance**. An ecosystem needs just the right amount of each thing. In this way, each living thing gets what it needs.

An eel is cleaned by a white-banded shrimp.

Macaque (muh-KAK) monkeys groom each other to get rid of unwanted insects.

Types of Ecosystems

There are many ecosystems. They fall into three main types: terrestrial, marine, and freshwater.

Terrestrial

Terrestrial ecosystems are on land. A desert is one example. There are many deserts on Earth. They are very hot and dry. They do not get much rain or snow.

The plants in deserts are often far apart. That is so each one can get the water it needs. The plants are smaller than those in wet areas. Small plants need less water. The animals in deserts can live with little water, too.

Animals in deserts are mainly reptiles and insects.

Zebras live in grasslands. A grassland is also a terrestrial ecosystem.

Other Ecosystems

Other terrestrial ecosystems include boreal (BOHR-ee-uhl) forests, grasslands, savannas, and tropical rainforests.

Many animals that live in the desert are nocturnal. This means they sleep during the day and are active at night.

Marine

Marine means "ocean." There is a lot of life in the ocean. Most ocean plants and animals live near the shore. There is a lot of food and light there. Tiny plants float in the water. Large plants grow on the seafloor. Sea animals eat the plants. Large sea animals eat the small animals. That is how energy from the sun moves through the system.

Other Marine Ecosystems

Other types of marine ecosystems include deep sea, open ocean, and estuary.

Continental shelf ecosystems are near the shore.

Estuaries are where rivers flow into oceans or seas.

Freshwater

Freshwater ecosystems include lakes and ponds. The water is calm there. Many plants and animals live near the shore. Others live deeper in the water. Large and small organisms swim and float in the water. Some small creatures even live in the mud at the bottom.

Water in freshwater ecosystems is not salty like ocean water.

Plants use energy from the sun. Animals eat the plants. Large animals eat the small animals. This is how they share the sun's energy.

Other Freshwater Ecosystems

Other freshwater ecosystems include rivers, streams, marshes, swamps, and wetlands.

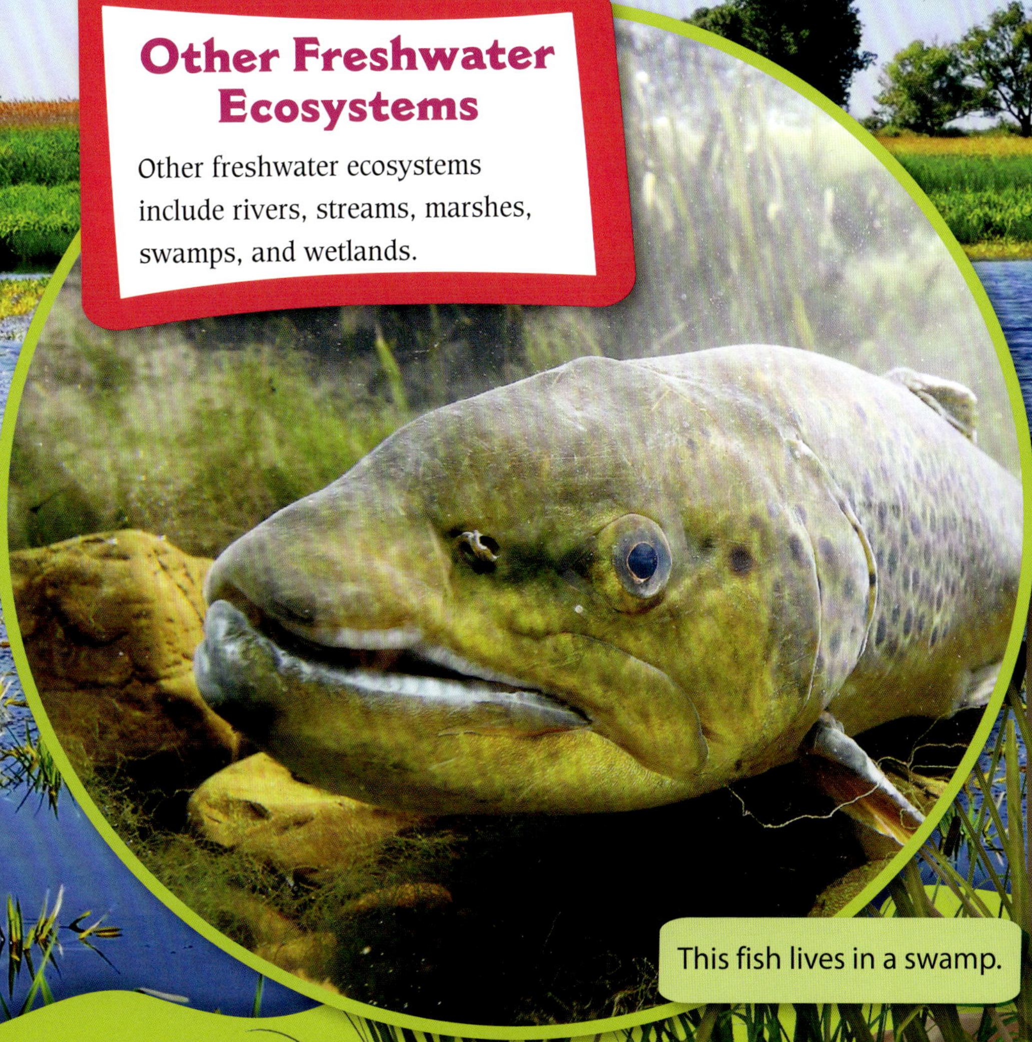

This fish lives in a swamp.

All Together

Balance is the key to a healthy ecosystem. Too much or too little of anything is a problem. Each thing must be there in just the right amount. That is balance.

There are things in nature that may change the balance. There may be a fire or a flood. There may be too much heat. Or there may be too little rain. But most often, people may cause a change. People may pollute the air. We may chop down too many trees. We may grow plants that do not belong there.

This beach is polluted with trash.

Living things count on us to care for their homes. We all live in one big ecosystem. Earth is their home. It is our home, too.

This scuba diver is careful as she swims with tropical fish.

Let's Do Science!

How can you change the balance of something? See for yourself!

What to Get

- coins
- masking tape
- marker
- paper clips
- small rocks
- yardstick or ruler

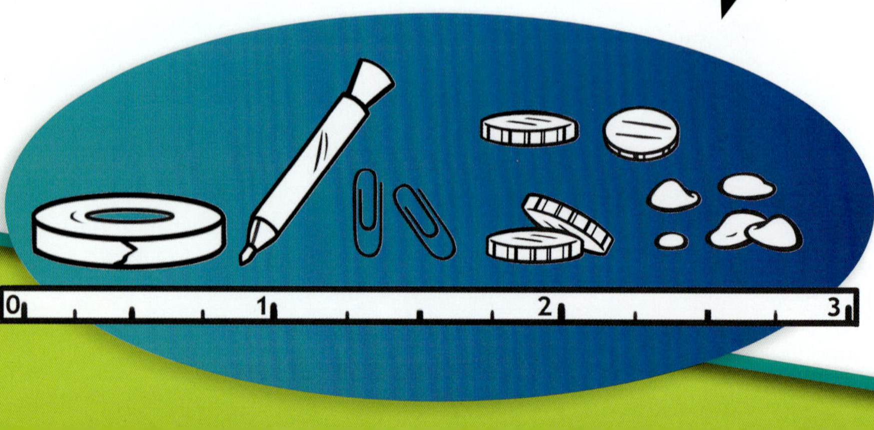

What to Do

1. Put tape on each end of the yardstick or ruler. Mark one side *A* and one side *B*.

2. Use your finger to find the balance point of the yardstick. Mark it with tape.

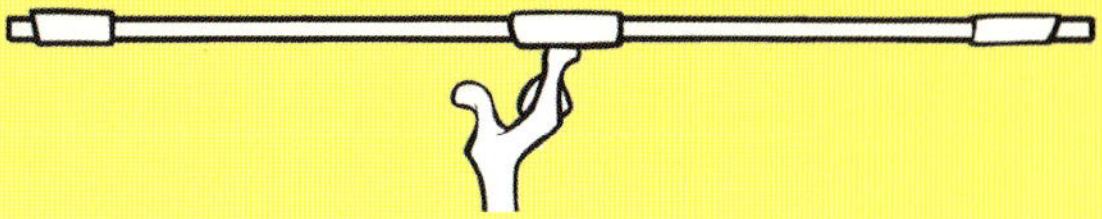

3. Tape a paper clip to side *A*. Find the new balance point.

4. Tape a coin to side *B*. Find the new balance point.

5. Tape a small rock to side *B*. Find the new balance point.

6. Tape more paper clips, coins, and rocks to each side until you find the center balance point again. How easy is it to change the balance of something?

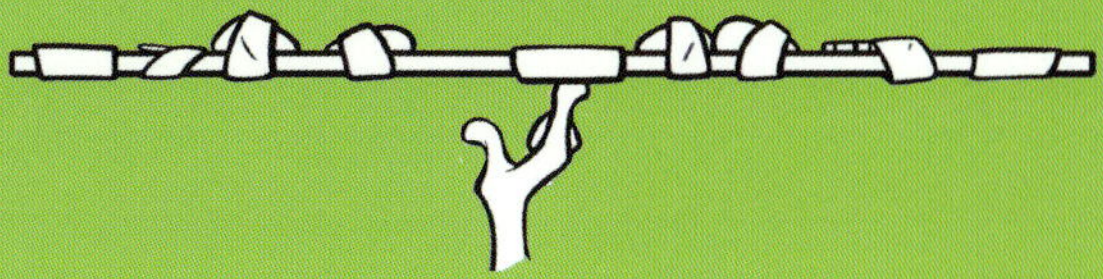

Glossary

balance—the state of things being in equal amounts or positions

condition—circumstance; the way that things are

consumers—organisms that eat plants, animals, or both

decomposers—organisms that break down and feed on dead plants and animals

ecosystem—everything that exists in a certain place

energy—power that can be used to do something

hierarchy—a way of organizing and ranking things, such as from small groups to larger groups

nutrients—substances that plants, animals, and people need to live and grow

organism—an individual living thing

producers—organisms that make their own food

Index

Your Turn!

Discover an Ecosystem

Find an area outdoors that has some plants. How many different plants do you see? Do you see any animals? Are there leaves and sticks on the ground? Move the leaves around. Look underneath. What do you see? Draw a picture of this small ecosystem.